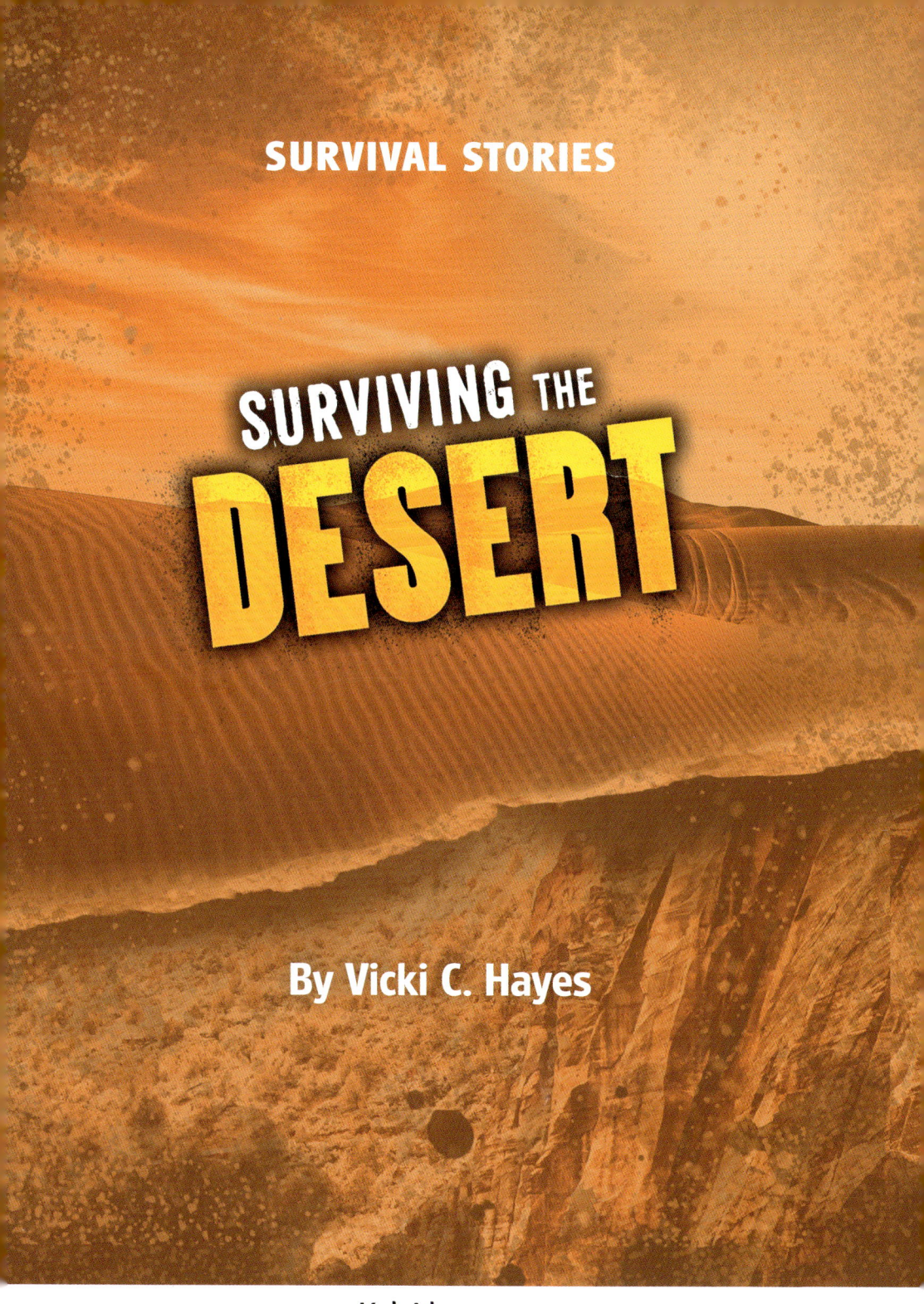

SURVIVAL STORIES

Surviving the Desert

By Vicki C. Hayes

Kaleidoscope
Minneapolis, MN

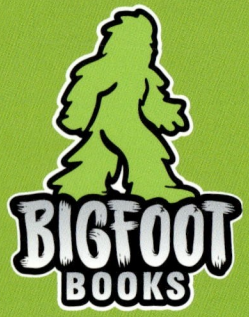

The Quest for Discovery Never Ends

....

This edition is co-published by agreement between Kaleidoscope and World Book, Inc.

Kaleidoscope Publishing, Inc.
6012 Blue Circle Drive
Minnetonka, MN 55343 U.S.A.

World Book, Inc.
180 North LaSalle St., Suite 900
Chicago IL 60601 U.S.A.

All rights reserved. No part of this book may be reproduced in any form without written permission from the publishers.

Kaleidoscope ISBNs
978-1-64519-206-0 (library bound)
978-1-64519-274-9 (ebook)

World Book ISBN
978-0-7166-4174-2 (library bound)

Library of Congress Control Number
2020936101

Text copyright © 2021 by Kaleidoscope Publishing, Inc. All-Star Sports, Bigfoot Books, and associated logos are trademarks and/or registered trademarks of Kaleidoscope Publishing, Inc.

Developed and produced by Focus Strategic Communications Inc.

Printed in the United States of America.

Bigfoot lurks within one of the images in this book. It's up to you to find him!

TABLE OF
CONTENTS

Survival Story 1: Freezing in the Desert 4

Survival Story 2: Wandering through the Wilderness 10

Survival Story 3: Sand Everywhere 16

Survival Story 4: Lose a Hand, Save a Life 22

Beyond the Book...28
Research Ninja..29
Further Resources...30
Glossary..31
Index 32
Photo Credits..32
About the Author..32

Survival Story 1
Freezing in the Desert

Victoria Grover heard coyotes howling in the distance. But she had made a fire to keep her safe and warm so she was not worried. In April 2012, she had gone on a hiking trip through the rocky cliffs and canyons of the Utah wilderness. On one of her hikes, Victoria lost track of time. She hoped to make it back to her car before dark. When she nearly fell over a 30-foot (9-m) cliff, she knew it was too dark to keep going.

The next morning, Victoria worked her way down a steep canyon. She lowered herself over several ledges. On the last one, she landed hard on a sharp rock. Victoria knew she had shattered several bones. She could not walk or even stand. She needed to be rescued.

The vast Utah wilderness is home to several dangerous animals. These include mountain lions, bears, and rattlesnakes.

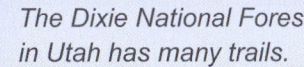
The Dixie National Forest in Utah has many trails.

WHAT IS A DESERT?

A desert is a biome with very little rainfall. The biggest desert is Antarctica with just 6.5 inches (16.5 cm) of precipitation a year. The largest hot desert is the Sahara. It is 3.5 million square miles (9.1 million sq km).

Deserts often have very clear and starry skies.

Victoria dragged herself 30 yards (27 m) to a stream. She got there as the sun went down. Temperatures dropped. She was too injured to gather firewood. She was going to be cold. She draped her thin **poncho** over her head. It helped, but she still shivered.

The next day, she yelled and banged rocks in the hope someone would hear her. The day after, she did the same. She spent four days with no food. Waves of hunger came and went.

Helicopters are commonly used in rescue missions in the desert.

FUN FACT
Temperatures in the desert range from more than 100 degrees Fahrenheit (38°C) in the daytime to below freezing at night.

The nights were when Victoria felt the worst. The cold never left her. It felt like she was in an icy lake and was not allowed out. The shivering exhausted her. She felt like she was doing pushups and she was not allowed to stop. On day five, Victoria stopped needing to pee. She knew this meant her body was shutting down.

That night, Victoria did not shiver. Her body could not do it anymore. She was getting **hypothermia**. She knew she would not survive another night. But on the morning of day six, a helicopter flew over her canyon. The pilot saw her waving and came to rescue her.

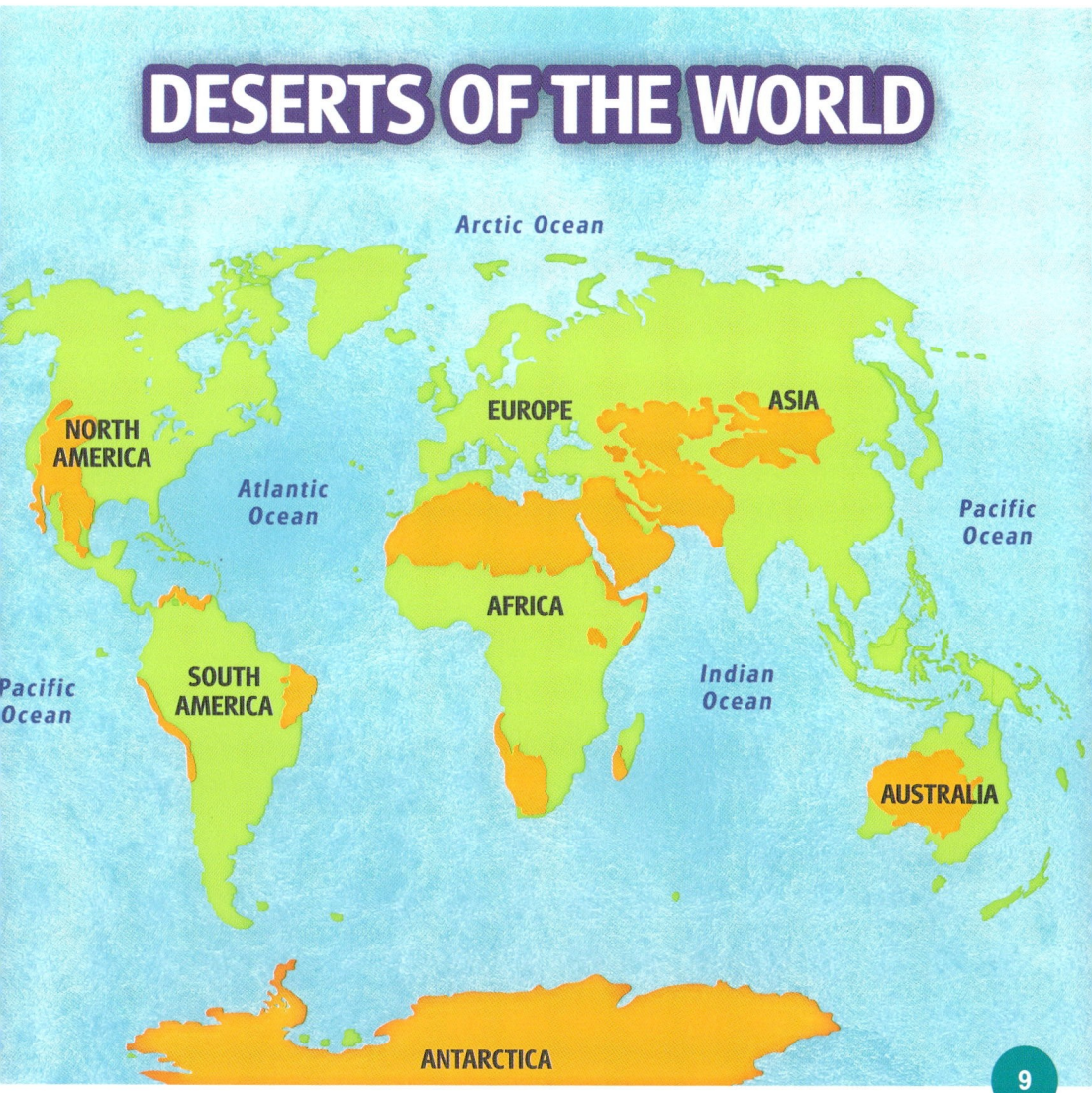

Survival Story 2
Wandering through the Wilderness

In 2016, Ann Rodgers' car ran out of gas on a dirt road in the Arizona desert. She was stranded. Her dog, Queenie, and cat, Nike, were in the back seat. She had some food and water, so she waited for help to come. At night, the temperature dropped. Ann and her pets huddled under a blanket. But no one came.

By the third day, Ann's water was gone. She left her cat, Nike, in the car with the window open. She packed whatever supplies she could find. Then, she and Queenie started walking.

The desert in Arizona is mountainous.

Ann Rodgers

The Fort Apache Reservation is located in Arizona.

They headed for a distant canyon with a creek. They followed the creek downstream. Ann's hunger started to grow. She and Queenie ate berries, dandelion greens, and clover. Once, Ann caught a turtle. She cooked it in its shell. It was her only protein except for bugs.

Ann climbed up and down ridges trying to get cell phone service until her battery died. Each night, she and Queenie huddled by the small fire she had made to stay warm. Each day, she carried burning **embers** wrapped in moss in case her lighter broke and she could not start a new fire.

HOW TO
MAKE A FIRE

Do not do this alone. Make sure an adult is helping.

GATHER MATERIALS

twigs sticks matches

CREATE A BASE

teepee log cabin pyramid

IGNITE THE FLAMES

oxygen helps the fire grow

Meanwhile, a search party formed. After eight days, they found Ann's car. Nike was still there. The cat was hungry, but healthy. However, searchers feared the worst for Ann. They knew there were bears and bobcats in the desert. They used **cadaver**-sniffing dogs to look for her remains.

Then, a search helicopter saw the word HELP spelled out in elk bones, sticks, and rocks. The pilot landed and was surprised when Queenie ran up to greet the helicopter. They found Ann around a bend in the canyon. She was badly sunburned, **malnourished**, and **dehydrated**. But her nine-day ordeal was over.

Ann's message could be seen from the air.

Ann was glad to finally be rescued after all her effort.

DANGERS IN THE DESERT

Some of the most dangerous creatures in the Arizona desert are scorpions, black bears, giant centipedes, poisonous spiders, Gila monsters, rattlesnakes, desert toads, and mountain lions.

Survival Story 3
Sand Everywhere

In 1994, Mauro Prosperi was competing in a 155-mile (250-km) race through the Sahara Desert in Africa. He was expecting the blistering sun and temperatures above 115 degrees Fahrenheit (46°C). He was not expecting a violent eight-hour sandstorm.

It was on the fourth day of the race that things went wrong. A yellow wall of swirling sand choked Mauro. The sand stung his skin like needles. He wrapped a towel around his face and kept moving. He did not want to be buried by the shifting sands. When the storm ended, he was lost.

The Sahara Race is a seven-day marathon race. Runners must carry all their own supplies on their backs.

Dust storms can make it hard to see or breathe in a desert.

Deserts can appear to go on forever.

Mauro drank his last bit of water. He used his urine to prepare his dehydrated food. He started walking. After two days, he came to a small **abandoned** building.

His food was gone, but he found a colony of bats. He ate 20 of them raw. He drank their blood. Then he saw a plane. It did not see him. He was miserable. Mauro hurt his wrist. But the extreme heat thickened his blood.

FUN FACT
Drinking blood can help with dehydration. Sailors have been known to drink turtle blood.

Mauro walked some more. He ate raw snakes, lizards, and mice. He sucked on wet wipes from his backpack. He licked morning dew off rocks. At night, he buried himself in the sand to stay warm.

On day eight, Mauro found a small waterhole. Gulping the water made him throw up. He had to take tiny sips for many hours. Then, he came across

Nomads live in tents instead of permanent houses.

a camp of **nomads**. They gave him goat's milk and went for help. After wandering for more than 180 miles (290 km) and losing 35 pounds (16 kg), Mauro was saved.

Nomadic families usually have animals and prepare food outdoors.

Survival Story 4
Lose a Hand, Save a Life

Aron Ralston was an experienced mountain climber. His climb into a Utah ravine should have been easy. But everything changed in an instant. On April 26, 2003, an 800-pound (360-kg) rock shifted, crushing his right hand. It pinned his arm against the canyon wall. Aron was trapped. For four days, he tried to get free. He chipped away at the rock with his pocketknife. He tried using his climbing gear to hoist the rock off his hand. Nothing worked.

Falling and shifting rocks can be dangerous for mountain climbers.

SURVIVING A DISASTER

Survivors often use flexible thinking. They know how to problem-solve. They accept the reality of their situation and search for options. They also tend to be optimistic and determined.

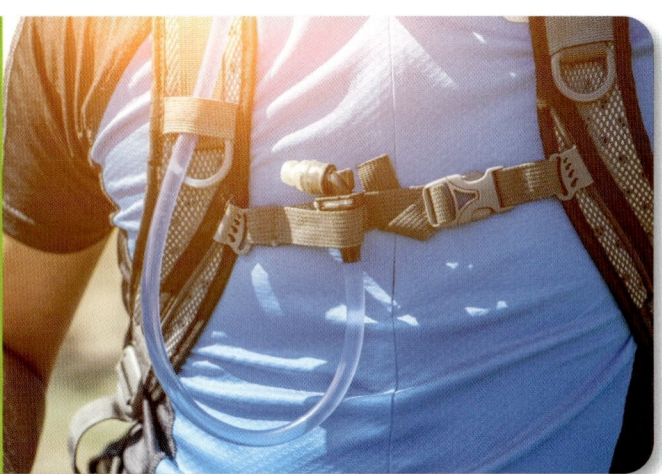

Mountain climbers need to drink a lot of water. They carry hydration packs on their backs. This leaves their hands free for climbing.

By now, Aron's food and water were gone. He was starving and dehydrated. At night, he worried about hypothermia. Then on day five, he decided on a drastic plan. He would cut off his hand. But his pocketknife was not sharp enough to cut through his arm bones. The plan failed. He recorded a good-bye video to his family. He carved his death date into the rock.

Then on day six, Aron had a new idea. He violently bent his arm until the bones snapped. Now, he could cut through his arm. Aron made a **tourniquet** using a rubber hose from his water pack. He started cutting.

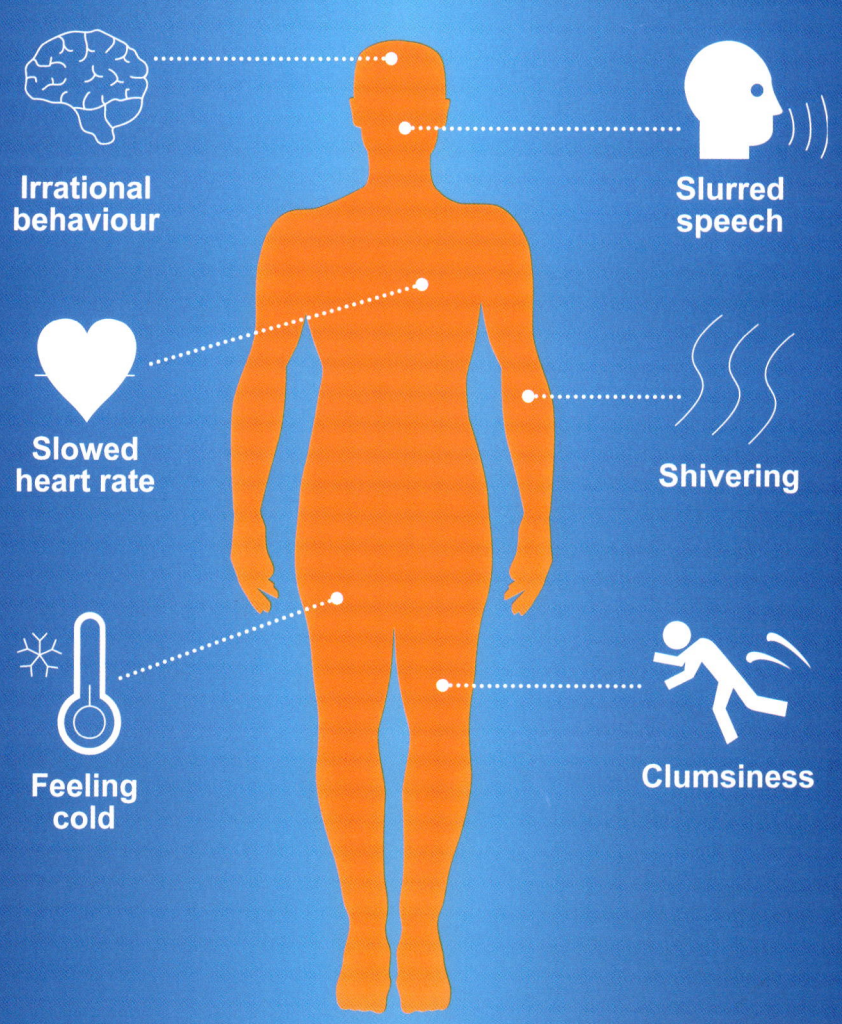

After an hour of horrible pain, Aron was free. He took a picture of his hand still trapped beneath the rock. Then he **rappelled** down a 60-foot (18-m) cliff to the canyon floor. Covered with blood, he hiked more than five miles (8 km).

Utah hikes can be beautiful, but they can also be dangerous.

Then, he met a family out hiking. The mom raced ahead to alert rescuers while the dad stayed with Aron. Soon, he was evacuated by helicopter. Aron lost his hand and 25 percent of his blood, but he kept his life.

FUN FACT

In 2010, a movie was made about Aron's ordeal. It was called *127 Hours*. James Franco played Aron.

Aron Ralston attended the premiere of *127 Hours* in New York.

BEYOND THE BOOK

After reading the book, it's time to think about what you learned. Try the following exercises to jumpstart your ideas.

THINK

DIFFERENT SOURCES. Think about what types of sources you could find about deserts. What could you find in an encyclopedia? What could you learn in other books? How could each of the sources be useful in its own way?

CREATE

PRIMARY SOURCES. A primary source is an original document, photograph, or interview. Make a list of primary sources you might be able to find about deserts. What new information might you learn from these sources?

SHARE

WHAT'S YOUR OPINION? Deserts can be very dangerous places. But some people think the challenge is worth the danger. They think it should be their choice whether they go out in dangerous places or not. Do you agree or disagree? Use evidence from the text to support your answer. Share your position and evidence with a friend. Does your friend agree with you?

GROW

REAL-LIFE RESEARCH. Think about what kinds of places you could visit to learn more about deserts. What other topics could you explore there?

RESEARCH NINJA

Visit *www.ninjaresearcher.com/2060* to learn how to take your research skills and book report writing to the next level!

RESEARCH

DIGITAL LITERACY TOOLS

SEARCH LIKE A PRO
Learn how to use search engines to find useful websites.

FACT OR FAKE?
Discover how you can tell a trusted website from an untrustworthy resource.

TEXT DETECTIVE
Explore how to zero in on the information you need most.

SHOW YOUR WORK
Research responsibly—learn how to cite sources.

WRITE

GET TO THE POINT
Learn how to express your main ideas.

PLAN OF ATTACK
Learn prewriting exercises and create an outline.

DOWNLOADABLE REPORT FORMS

Further Resources

BOOKS

Franchino, Vicky. *Sahara Desert*. North Mankato, MN: Lake Publishing, 2016.

Goldish, Meish. *Lost in a Desert*. New York, NY: Bearport Publishing, 2015.

Silverman, Buffy. *Let's Visit the Desert*. Minneapolis, MN: Lerner, 2016.

WEBSITES

Factsurfer.com gives you a safe, fun way to find more information.

1. Go to www.factsurfer.com.
2. Enter "Surviving the Desert" into the search box and click 🔍
3. Select your book cover to see a list of related websites.

Glossary

abandoned: To be given up on or left completely alone. When someone is stuck in the wilderness with no help, they can feel abandoned.

cadaver: A dead body. Rescue dogs find living people, but cadaver dogs find human flesh that is decomposing.

dehydrated: The loss of a large amount of water. Food is dehydrated to make it lighter to carry, but dehydration in people can cause death.

embers: Small pieces of burning or glowing wood. If embers can be carried safely, they can be used to start a new fire when there are no matches available.

hypothermia: A condition in which the body's temperature is dangerously low. When someone in cold weather appears confused or drowsy, they may have hypothermia.

malnourished: People who have low amounts of the vitamins and minerals necessary for life in their bodies.

nomads: People who travel from place to place. Nomads carry tents, food, and all their supplies with them as they move.

poncho: A lightweight piece of cloth with a hole in the middle for the head. Many hikers wear plastic ponchos to protect themselves and their gear from rain.

rappelled: Moved down a vertical rock using ropes. The climbers first attached their ropes to a rock, and then they rappelled down the steep cliff.

tourniquet: A device used to completely stop the flow of blood. Tourniquets are often used to control excessive bleeding that could be life-threatening.

Index

127 Hours, 27
Antarctica, 5, 9
bats, 19
dehydration, 14, 18, 19, 24
Fort Apache Reservation, 12
Franco, James, 27
Grover, Victoria, 4, 6, 7, 8, 9
hypothermia, 9, 24, 25
Nike, 10, 14

nomads, 20, 21
Prosperi, Mauro, 16, 8, 19, 20, 21
Queenie, 10, 12, 14
Ralston, Aron, 22, 24, 26, 27
Rodgers, Ann, 10, 11, 12, 14, 15
Sahara Desert, 5, 16
Sahara Race, 16
Utah, 4, 5, 22, 26

PHOTO CREDITS

The images in this book are reproduced through the courtesy of: Fotokina/Shutterstock Images, front cover, (top background), p. 1 (top); Ivana Casanova/Shutterstock Images, front cover (skulls); Cire notrevo/Shutterstock Images, front cover (bottom), p. 1; Christina Moraes/Shutterstock Images, p. 4; Atmosphere1/Shutterstock Images, p. 5; Susan Schmitz/Shutterstock Images, p. 6 (top); Gabriela Beres/Shutterstock Images, p. 6 (bottom); Daxiao Productions/Shutterstock Images, p. 7; Maria Jeffs/Shutterstock Images, p. 8; Ingrid Curry/Shutterstock Images, pp. 10-11(top); Astrid Galvan/AP Images, pp. 10-11 (bottom); Goldilock Project/Shutterstock Images, p. 12 (top); ChristianChan/Shutterstock Images, p. 12 (bottom); INelson/Shutterstock Images, p. 13 (match box); Tartila/Shutterstock Images, p. 13 (lit fire); Arizona Department of Public Safety/AP Images, p. 14, 15 (top); Eric Isselee/Shutterstock Images, p. 15 (bottom); Oscar Carrascosa Martinez/Shutterstock Images, p. 16; PIERRE VERDY/AFP/Getty Images, p. 17; Dmitry Pichugin/Shutterstock Images, p. 18; FJAH/Shutterstock Images, p. 19; ingehogenbijl/Shutterstock Images, p. 20; Torsten Pursche/Shutterstock Images, p. 21 (goat); federico neri/Shutterstock Images, p. 21 (nomad); VagnerAndras/Shutterstock Images, p. 22; Aron Ralston/CC BY-SA 3.0, pp. 22-23; dimid_86/Shutterstock Images, p. 24; bc21/Shutterstock Images, p. 25 (human body); dcabb/Shutterstock Images, p. 26; Charles Eshelman/FilmMagic/Getty Images, p. 27.

About the Author

Vicki C. Hayes lives and works in Seattle with her husband, dog, and four nearby grandchildren. She loves all types of hiking but is careful not to get lost.